Shake. Stir. Sip.

Shake.
Stir.
Sip.

MORE THAN

50

EFFORTLESS
COCKTAILS
MADE IN
EQUAL PARTS

Kara Newman

Photographs by John Lee

CHRONICLE BOOKS
SAN FRANCISCO

Text copyright © 2016 by Kara Newman.
Photographs copyright © 2016 by Chronicle Books LLC.

Library of Congress Cataloging-in-Publication Data
Names: Newman, Kara, author.
Title: Shake. stir. sip. / Kara Newman.
Description: San Francisco : Chronicle Books, 2016. / Includes index.
Identifiers: LCCN 2015044160 | ISBN 9781452152479 (hardcover : alk. paper)
Subjects: LCSH: Cocktails. | LCGFT: Cookbooks.
Classification: LCC TX951 .N547 2016 | DDC 641.87/4–dc23 LC record
  available at http://lccn.loc.gov/2015044160

Manufactured in China

Designed by Alice Chau .
Photographs by John Lee
Drink styling by Eric Passetti & Will Herrera

10 9 8 7 6 5 4 3 2

Chronicle Books LLC
680 Second Street
San Francisco, California 94107
www.chroniclebooks.com

Contents

Introduction

I've been obsessed with "equal parts" cocktails for a long time. At first, I didn't know that they were a category of drinks. I just knew that they were impossible to screw up.

If you've never had (or made) one before, an equal-parts drink is just what it sounds like: A drink made with ingredients measured out in precisely equal proportions.

The first drink to hit my "equal parts" radar screen was the Negroni: gin, sweet vermouth, and crimson Campari. I'm probably not alone in that—the drink has had an amazing ascent over the past few years.

But once I started looking around, I couldn't believe how many cocktails measure out this way—why hadn't I noticed it before? From the four-part box step of the Last Word (gin, lime juice, Maraschino liqueur, and Green Chartreuse) to the aptly named 50-50 martini

(equal parts gin and vermouth), equal-parts drinks have long been part of the classic cocktail canon, and modern-day bartenders love them too.

And why not? After years of fussy, baroque cocktails, simplicity is back in style. We want easy elegance, streamlined recipes that work every time.

Let me be clear, "easy" doesn't mean "dumbed down." Just ask any bartender who has tried to create an original equal-parts drink; finding that perfect balance can present quite a challenge. But once it's achieved, it's like magic. It just *works*.

The secret weapon? Ratios. For many (including me), a lightbulb goes on the minute you realize that cooking is all about ratios. Many sauces, for example, build on basic ratios, like one-part butter to one-part flour in a roux. Baking, too, has its ratios; the classic pound cake takes its name from early recipes that call for one pound each of butter, sugar, egg, and flour.

The same holds true of cocktails. This book focuses on drinks that have equal-parts ratios, just like a roux or a pound cake recipe. Houston, Texas-based bartender Bobby Heugel terms them "equinox drinks"—cocktails made in perfectly equal proportions, similar to the equinox days when hours of daylight and darkness fall in equal measure. Some drinks also allow for a dash of bitters or a squeeze of citrus, but the basis is always the equal-parts template.

These templates aren't necessarily set in stone. They're a starting point, meant to be used, tweaked to your preference (adding or subtracting sweetness, for example), or built upon with garnishes and dashes and spritzes.

I wasn't surprised to find that some bartenders utilize these templates as teaching tools. "We start with drinks that are 1:1—drinks made with two ingredients in equal proportion—then drinks with three parts, then four parts," explains Scottsdale, Arizona-based mixologist Jason Asher. "Once you understand the bloodlines, the families, it's easier to understand how to make drinks."

Another score for the equal-parts drink; they are a breeze to measure and mix, for one or for many. Wherever possible, I've noted where drinks can be easily scaled up to serve a group, and the section on party planning (see page 26) is designed to help kick up your cocktail game for gatherings. (Self-promo alert: If you're craving still more advice on big-batch drinks, I hope you'll consider picking up a copy of my other book, *Cocktails for a Crowd*.)

Give these drinks a spin, and you'll see why the Negroni has captured bartenders' imaginations—along with other equal-parts cocktails.

Stocking the Equal-Parts Bar

LIQUOR CABINET

Whether you're building a bar from scratch or just adding a few well-chosen bottles to an existing collection, here's a guide to spirits called for throughout this book. I've called out a few brands I recommend for mixing in cocktails, but this is by no means a comprehensive list. (You can also view my ratings on *Wine Enthusiast*'s website if you're seeking a deeper-dive into brands and tasting notes.)

MUST-HAVE BASE SPIRITS

Brandy

Brandy comes in a very wide range of prices and provenances. The only guideline in my mind is to get one that you enjoy sipping straight up, and it will make your mixed drinks wonderful, too.

Cognac is the classic brandy, made in France's Cognac region, and a value-priced VSOP (basically, a brandy that's in the middle of the age range, delicious but not too old/rare to mix) is a useful building block for a bar, although I wouldn't turn my nose up at a well-made **American brandy** either. Meanwhile, **Calvados**, Normandy's apple brandy, and America's applejack both are delicious but I'd keep them on the nice-to-have list.

Recommended brands: Cognac Ferrand, Germain-Robin

Gin

You can't go wrong with a bottle of **dry gin**. London Dry Gin is the most common type you'll find, noted for its pronounced juniper note. But other types of dry gin exist, such as New Western or

New American gin, a style that showcases other botanicals (like citrus peels, spices, or herbs), usually made by producers in North America, including many smaller craft producers. If you prefer an earthier, more neutral style with as little juniper as possible, **Plymouth gin** is the way to go (and in this book, "gin" versus "dry gin" means feel free to choose either style). Finally, lightly sweetened **Old Tom Gin** is called for in one recipe in this book. Whatever gin you choose, don't skimp. A good gin should appeal to you enough to drink in a well-chilled, minimally adorned martini.

Recommended brands: Tanqueray London Dry Gin, Haymans Old Tom Gin

Rum

White rum and **dark rum** (aged rum) are staples. The former (it's barrel aged, but the color is filtered out) is ideal for mixing Mojitos and other summery drinks, while dark rum (which spends more time in the barrel and takes on gorgeous caramel and toffee tones) is great for straight-up sipping and mixing into tropical drinks. **Gold rum** (generally aged longer than white rum and shorter than dark rum) is nice to have for rounding out a collection, and has more honey and vanilla flavor compared to the deeper, richer caramel of a dark rum.

Recommended brands: Caña Brava (white rum), Zacapa (aged rum)

Tequila

Try to get over whatever horrible shooters you knocked back during spring break in college. Tequila for grown-ups should be made from 100 percent agave, and can have delicious notes of agave nectar and spice. **Blanco** (unaged or minimally aged) tequila is a must-have for margaritas and more. Barrel-aged **reposado** tequila is nice to have, and adds lovely vanilla and caramel notes to the mix.

Recommended brands: Siete Leguas, Tapatio

Vodka

Clean, neutral, and extremely versatile, vodka can be made from any base, although grain and potato vodkas are most often seen, and can be made in any country.

Recommended brands: Absolut Elyx, Karlsson's (potato vodka)

Whiskey

Four different types are called for in this book, although others certainly exist. Among the American whiskeys, **rye** and **bourbon** are staples you'll use again and again. Rye whiskey is a bit leaner and spicier, where bourbon, made with corn, is a bit sweeter. In a pinch, you can sub one for another in a drink recipe, though you'll end up with slightly different flavor profiles. **Scotch whisky** is made in Scotland. Save the pricey single malt Scotches for sipping straight up, and use a blended Scotch for cocktail recipes. Just beware that some Scotches can be aggressively smoky—which is fine, if that's what you want in your drink. Finally, **Irish whiskey** is made

in Ireland, and tends to be light, grassy, and fruity. It blends well with simple mixers like ginger ale as well as sipping nicely alone.

Recommended brands: Rittenhouse Rye, Buffalo Trace Bourbon, Jameson Irish Whiskey

NICE-TO-HAVE BASE SPIRITS

Some will argue that these are must-haves, but I find that I use them less often or in smaller quantities than the bottles previously mentioned.

- Absinthe
- Aquavit
- Cachaça
- Calvados
- Mezcal
- Pisco
- Soju

MUST-HAVE LIQUEURS

Amaro

Several *amari* are mentioned throughout this book. You don't need to run out and acquire all of these herbal, often bitter Italian liqueurs, but it's good to have a bottle on hand. I'd recommend selecting one that's only moderately bitter: Amaro Montenegro, Amaro Nonino, Meletti Amaro, and Averna all are good choices. Fernet is more intensely bitter. Some people love it, but I consider it a nice-to-have item.

Campari: Also technically an amaro, since it's Italian and bitter, but its vibrant red hue makes it stand out. Plus, it's a must-have for Negronis.

Orange Liqueur

Cointreau is a go-to ingredient for sweetening and adding orange flavor to drinks. If you have room for a second one, the less-sweet Ferrand Dry Curaçao also is excellent. Blue curaçao also has an orange flavor; the blue hue makes it a fun novelty, and it's nice to have but not 100 percent necessary.

NICE-TO-HAVE LIQUEURS

These liqueurs are helpful modifiers for cocktails, meaning that they add distinctive flavor in addition to base spirits like gin or whiskey. If you have even one or two of the following bottles, it greatly expands the range of drinks you can make, though you'll likely use them in small quantities.

- Aperol
- Benedictine
- Crème de cacao (dark or white)
- Crème de menthe
- Crème de pêche
- Crème de violette
- Cynar
- Domaine de Canton, or another ginger liqueur
- Fernet
- Green Chartreuse or Yellow Chartreuse (or both)
- Maraschino liqueur
- St-Germain elderflower liqueur

MUST-HAVE WINES, VERMOUTHS, AND FORTIFIED/APERITIF WINES

Just to clarify what's what: Vermouth is wine fortified (usually) with a small amount of brandy and aromatized with herbs or spices. Aperitif wines also are fortified, and some have additional flavorings (like citrus peels) added. Sherry is also a fortified wine, made specifically with grapes grown in or near the town of Jerez de la Frontera in Spain.

A note on all of the following: Fortified or not, be sure to store wines in the refrigerator once they are opened. Fortified wines will last longer than non-fortified types, but do try to use them as quickly as possible; most will keep up to a month, but after that may develop "off" flavors.

Dry Vermouth

Also known as white vermouth, and a critical martini ingredient.

Recommended brands: Dolin Blanc, Noilly Prat

Sweet Vermouth

Also known as red vermouth, and key for Negronis and many other drinks.

Recommended brands: Carpano Antica, Punt e Mes, Dolin Rouge

Sparkling Wine

Whether your taste runs to Italy's Prosecco, Spain's cava, France's Champagne, or domestic sparklers, it's very helpful to have a bottle of bubbly on hand for topping up a wide range of drinks (or drinking by itself, if you're feeling festive).

NICE-TO-HAVE WINES, VERMOUTHS, AND FORTIFIED/APERITIF WINES

Aperitif Wines

Both Lillet Blanc and Cocchi Americano are excellent upgrades to dry vermouth, while Cocchi Torino, Lillet Rouge, or Bonal are ideal red-wine aperitifs. All of these add dimension to cocktails but also drink very well unadulterated.

Sake

This rice-based alcoholic beverage isn't technically a wine, but it has lower alcohol like one, and it's fermented (like wine or beer) but not distilled (like liquor).

Sherry

For cocktails (and the occasional dessert sipper), it's helpful to have a bottle or two of sherry on hand. Although sherry comes in a wide range of styles, consider acquiring one bottle of **dry sherry** (such as fino or manzanilla) and one **sweet sherry** (such as oloroso).

BITTERS

Bitters are essentially tinctures made with herbs, roots, spices, bittering agents such as gentian or wormwood, and other flavorings. Some experts like to describe bitters as "the salt and pepper" of cocktails, meaning that they "season" drinks with just enough bitterness to help round them out, without adding too much perceptible flavor.

In context of a book about drinks made with ingredients in equal proportions, bitters are used in such minute amounts—usually just a couple of dashes—that it makes sense to include them. They don't quite fit the "equal parts" structure, but they don't interrupt the integrity of the drinks, either, and can add considerable complexity.

If you're starting a bar from scratch, you'll want to invest in Angostura bitters, which has a spiced flavor profile, and orange bitters, such as Regan's Orange Bitters No. 6. Tiny amounts are used in drinks, so the bottles tend to last a very long time.

If you're interested in filling out your bar with additional bitters, consider adding Peychaud's, which has cherry-and-spice notes and is called for in classic cocktails (such as a La Louisiane, page 54); chocolate mole bitters, which blend particularly well into tequila-based drinks (and is mighty delicious in coffee, too); and celery bitters, which give gin-based drinks a sprightly vegetal kick and can be dashed into Bloody Mary variations as well.

Throughout this book, when a bartender recommended a particular type of bitters, I've left the name and type intact. The bitters can be omitted and it won't ruin the drink. However, adding the right bitters only makes the drink better.

A final, equal-parts-friendly note on bitters: If you have both Angostura and orange bitters on hand, you can combine them together—in equal measures, of course—to create your own "house bitters," a secret weapon used at a great many high-end bars.

SODA WATER, SELTZER, AND OTHER CARBONATED WATERS

Another exception to the equal parts rule is fizzy water, such as club soda or seltzer. Often, just a splash of carbonated water is added to a drink to lighten it a bit, particularly for drinks made with relatively viscous, strong-flavored ingredients, like Campari or some fruit juices. It's also a matter of taste—some people enjoy a lot of carbonation, while others prefer just a little. Of course, it's also a matter of how much room is in your glass, since glass sizes can vary widely.

Club Soda

Artificially carbonated water to which sodium salts and/or potassium salts have been added is called *club soda*. This is done to mimic the effect of bubbly mineral water, but the salts also are added to neutralize acidity in some water. In these cocktail recipes, you can use either club soda or soda water/seltzer—it's a matter of personal preference—and the stronger flavors of other ingredients likely will overpower the nuances of sparkling waters anyway.

Mineral Water

Flat or sparkling water from a mineral spring is referred to as *mineral water*. If it's carbonated, that's naturally occurring. Most of these waters contain some degree of mineral content (hence the name), including salt, and since it's derived from a natural source, the flavor, saltiness, and amount of carbonation can vary widely.

Soda Water

A catch-all term for carbonated water used throughout the book, "soda water" refers to seltzer, which is artificially carbonated water with no minerals added to it. It was the term mixologists used in the late 1800s, when many now-classic cocktail recipes were created. They would have used glass siphons to create carbonation; now we have access to plenty of bottled seltzers as well as home carbonating devices like the SodaStream.

Tonic Water

A sweetened soft drink made with carbonated water, tonic water is a key cocktail mixer—included in highballs like the classic gin and tonic (see page 42). An important note: Tonic water is NOT interchangeable with soda water, seltzer, or club soda since it adds perceptible sweetness and a slightly bitter edge.

TOOLS

Only a few very useful tools are needed to make good cocktails. Here's a short-list of gear to get.

Citrus Squeezer

This tool isn't absolutely necessary—unless you're making drinks for a large group and need a LOT of lemon or lime juice—but it sure is nice to have, because it often extracts more juice than squeezing wedges by hand. Look for a hand-held squeezer or press in stainless steel or enamel.

Cocktail Shaker

For shaken drinks, choose either a two-piece Boston shaker (which most bartenders choose) or three-piece cobbler shaker (which has a strainer built in), depending on what you prefer. Either way, a shaker that holds about 16 oz [480 ml] is small enough to handle if you're making a single drink and large enough to double up if you're shaking for two.

Jigger

Perhaps the single most important tool in the equal-parts arsenal, a jigger ensures precision in measuring out liquids. Since they come in an array of sizes, be sure to check how many ounces or millilitres your jigger holds on each side before using it. For a starter bar, a jigger that holds ½ oz [15 ml] on one side and 1 oz [30 ml] on the other should meet most measuring needs. A second jigger with a full 2-oz [60-ml] measure is a helpful accompaniment.

Long-Handled Spoon

Perfect for reaching down into the bottom of a mixing glass or pitcher to stir thoroughly.

Mixing Glass

For stirred drinks, any large glass vessel or pitcher can be used, although a mixing glass is intended for stirring drinks with ice. Some have spouts to make for easy pouring. For most mixing needs, the 16-oz [480-ml] pint glass that comes in a two-piece shaker will do the trick. For a more decorative touch, a 19-oz [570-ml] cut-glass Yarai mixing glass is beautiful, and that's what you'll see at many upscale bars.

Muddler

A muddler usually has a blunt or rounded edge, like a mini baseball bat, meant for crushing herbs, spices, or other ingredients. The back of a spoon also can be used in a pinch.

Paring Knife

Odds are you already have one in your kitchen. It's invaluable for cutting garnishes, too.

Peeler

Again, you likely already have one, and it's useful for peeling off thick pieces of citrus peel for garnishes. Many bartenders prefer a Y-shaped vegetable peeler for even faster, more precise garnish needs.

Strainer

A Hawthorne bar strainer is flat and equipped with a spring coil, so it fits neatly into a mixing glass to catch ice from falling into a drink.

GLASSES

A wide range of glasses are referenced throughout this book. If you don't own the "right" glasses, don't worry, just use what seems to fit the drink best. Glassware sizes can vary widely depending on the manufacturer—these are just general guidelines.

Collins

A tall, straight up-and-down glass with plenty of room for ice, named for the Tom Collins cocktail. Holds 10 to 14 oz [300 to 420 ml]. Highball glasses may be substituted.

Coupe

A stemmed glass with a rounded, saucer-like bowl, commonly used for classic cocktails. Martini glasses may be substituted.

Highball

This is the most common bar glass, a straight up-and-down model that usually holds 8 to 12 oz [240 to 360 ml] used for anything from Bloody Marys to gin and tonics. The larger collins glass may be substituted.

Margarita

This curvy, stemmed glass is used for margaritas and daiquiris, but the martini glass or a large red wine goblet may be substituted.

Martini

A stemmed glass with a V-shaped bowl, the martini is the classic vessel for any drink served without ice—but especially, martinis! Small martinis—the kind once served at fabled "three-martini lunches"— may hold 3 to 5 oz [90 to 150 ml], mid-size martini glasses hold up to 9 oz [270 ml], and larger martini glasses might hold even more than that, usually topping out at 12 oz [360 ml], although that's a tremendous amount of liquid for a single drink, and it's not seen very often.

Nick and Nora

A relatively new addition to the glassware canon, this smallish glass with a narrow bowl usually holds 5 to 6 oz [150 to 180 ml]; a coupe or small (white) wine glass may be substituted.

Rocks

Also called an old-fashioned glass, this short, straight glass typically holds 4 to 8 oz [120 to 240 ml], and is the standard glass used for drinks mixed with ice.

Wine Goblet or Wine Glass

A standard white wine glass holds from 6 to 12 oz [180 to 360 ml], while the larger and more rounded red wine glass may hold anywhere from 8 to 24 oz [240 to 720 ml].

GARNISHES

When your drinks are this stream-lined, consider it an opportunity to get creative with your garnishes. Ideally, these decorative touches should not only add visual interest, creating a contrasting or comple-mentary pop of color to your drink, they should add a pleasing aroma, too. Some—like cucumber wheels or olives—also add a hint of flavor to a cocktail, and are ideal for nib-bling once the drink is gone.

In a variety of forms from wheels to twists, citrus garnishes are almost always the perfect accessory for a well-dressed drink.

NOTE: If you're making drinks for a party, prepare garnishes ahead of time—one garnish per glass, and do it as close to service time as you can manage.

Peels

Use a knife or vegetable peeler to cut a swath of zest from the fruit. Many bartenders encourage using the serving glass for inspiration. Cut wide pieces of peel for sturdy vessels like rocks glasses and thinner pieces for graceful coupes or champagne flutes.

Twists

Use a knife or vegetable peeler to cut strips approximately 1 in [2.5 cm] wide and 4 in [10 cm] long. Cut each strip lengthwise to produce narrow 4-in [10-cm] strips about ½ in [12 mm] wide. Wind each around your finger-tip into a circle and secure with a toothpick. Cover the twists with a damp paper towel. When you're ready to serve drinks, remove the toothpicks and discard. Gently pull the twists to unfurl them.

Wedges

For wedges, cut lemons or limes into quarters. Cut oranges into eighths.

Wheels

Cut the ends off a lemon, lime, orange, or cucumber and discard.

Slice into rounds about ¼ in [6 mm] thick.

If the wheel will be perched on the edge of the glass, cut a slit from the center of the citrus or cucumber to the outer peel.

Brandied Cherries

Spear them on toothpicks to garnish drinks like the La Louisane (page 54) and the Bijou (page 70), although they're great for pretty much any whiskey-based drink. This recipe has become my go-to when fresh cherries are unavailable. Dried, pitted Bing cherries plump up when soaked in syrup made with brandy (or bourbon, aged rum, or other brown spirit). A dash of almond or vanilla extract mimics the flavor usually imparted by the cherry pits. (As an alternative to DIY brandied cherries, you can also purchase a reputable brand of commerical maraschino cherries, such as Luxardo. But skip the chemical-laden, bright-red orbs found in the supermarket, please.)

In a small saucepan over medium heat, combine ½ cup [100 g] sugar and ½ cup [120 ml] water. Bring to a rolling boil, stirring until the sugar is dissolved. Lower the heat to a simmer and stir in ¼ tsp almond extract and ½ cup [100 g] dried cherries. Allow to simmer, uncovered, for 5 to 7 minutes. Remove from the heat, add ½ cup [120 ml] brandy, such as Cognac, and let cool. Transfer the cherries to a mason jar or other container with a lid. Add more brandy to cover the cherries if needed. Store in the refrigerator for up to 2 weeks.

More Tips and Techniques

CHILLING GLASSES

This is one of the easiest techniques possible, which bars employ all the time to elevate their drinks. All that's needed is to place your glass in the freezer. That's it. If possible, place glassware in the freezer for about 30 minutes before making drinks for a full-on frosty effect that looks great and keeps the drink chilled as long as possible. If you've forgotten to plan ahead, place the glass in the freezer and start making the drink, then fish it out when you're ready to pour. Even 5 minutes makes a noticeable difference.

Chilling a glass is less important if you're making a drink served on the rocks—in other words, if ice will be in the glass, it will serve to keep the drink cold. But for a drink that's strained and served "up"—without ice—a chilled glass makes a big difference in keeping the drink as cold as possible for as long as possible.

CREATING A "FLOAT"

To "float" a liquid on top of a drink, hold a metal spoon upside down, directly over the drink. Slowly pour the liquid over the back of the spoon, so it gently cascades over the spoon, settling on top of the drink. If done correctly, the liquid should "float" on top of the drink in a separate layer. This technique is used in the Sangarita (page 56).

MAKING SIMPLE SYRUP

Used to sweeten drinks, simple syrup is the bartender's secret weapon. In a small saucepan, combine equal parts sugar and water. Set over high heat, stirring until the sugar is dissolved. When the liquid starts to boil, turn the heat to low, and simmer for 10 minutes. Remove from the heat and let cool to room temperature. Decant into a mason jar (or other small container with a lid) and store in the refrigerator for up to 10 days.

MUDDLING

Use a muddler—a blunt tool made of wood or plastic—or a wooden spoon inside a cocktail shaker or pitcher to gently crush herbs or release juices from pieces of fruit or vegetables. This technique is used in the Blood Orange Caipirinha (page 48) and the Cucumber Gimlet (page 72), among others.

A GUIDE TO ICE FOR COCKTAILS

As a key ingredient in any cocktail, ice plays a dual role: It chills a drink and provides dilution as it melts. What type of ice should you use for your drink? That depends on how much dilution you want.

And for drinks where the ice isn't strained out of the drink, you'll also want to consider how the ice looks in the finished drink.

NOTE: Ice can pick up odors or flavors, so be cognizant of what's in your freezer—you may not want to place an ice-cube tray directly next to, say, fish from last night's dinner. Additionally, some bartenders recommend using purified water for the most neutral ice possible.

Crushed Ice

Often used for tropical-style drinks, crushed ice means that the ice is broken into very small pieces, so it melts very quickly. It's used in particularly boozy drinks, where that extra dilution is desirable if not downright necessary, and in drink styles where a "snowy" appearance to the ice is preferred. Crushing ice is easy—and fun—to do. Place ice cubes in a clean tea towel, resealable plastic bag (squeeze out the air), or a Lewis bag (a heavy-duty canvas bag designed specifically for crushing ice). Using a meat mallet or wooden rolling pin, BANG on the ice to break it into small pieces. Since crushed ice melts rapidly, it can't be prepared ahead of time if you're making drinks for a group. Luckily, it's plenty entertaining to watch someone crush ice. Try it in the Parisian Blonde (page 76), Cran-Brandy Cobbler (page 98), or Rum Punch (page 122).

Cubes

Basic ice cubes—approximately 1 by 1 in [2.5 by 2.5 cm]—can be scooped into a cocktail shaker for chilling drinks, or directly into a glass for drinks served "on the rocks." They'll melt at a moderate rate, adding a desirable amount of water for a booze-forward drink. There's no need to be too precious about the ice—standard ice-cube trays will do the trick. However, if you want to take things to the next level, invest in a silicone tray for perfectly square cubes that mimic the ones bars make using Kold-Draft or other fancy ice machines.

Large Cubes or Spheres

Regular ice cubes can be used, but larger pieces of ice provide an aesthetically pleasing, fancy touch for drinks served "on the rocks," as well as for savoring straight-up spirits pours like whiskey or brandy. These large, super-slow-melting shapes can be made using silicone molds. Be sure to make them well ahead of serving so they have sufficient time to freeze, and check that the cube will fit into your glassware. Some bartenders deliberately drape citrus peels over these large cubes, just to accentuate the shape. Try it in the Old Pal (see page 61), Sin Cyn (page 66), or Toffee Negroni (page 62).

Punch-Bowl Ice

These large blocks or other shapes are the slowest-melting of all, designed to chill large quantities of liquid without diluting too quickly. (For directions on how to make punch-bowl ice, see page 28.)

Party-Planning Tips

Even with the most carefully chosen cocktails, a few guidelines will help keep your entertaining plans as stress-free as possible.

Make a list, check it twice. Figure out exactly which liquors you'll need and how much of each, and also the mixers, ice, garnishes, tools, and glassware. And don't forget your cleanup gear, such as dish towels, paper towels, and trash bins. (If a sink isn't in easy reach, many bartenders recommend one trash bin for ice and liquids and a second bin for "dry" trash.)

Don't forget the ice! But how much is enough? I rely on this formula from Portland, Oregon, bartender Kelley Swenson. For each 750 ml of cocktail (the size of a standard bottle of liquor), he allots 7 lb [3.2 kg] of ice. "And then I add extra," Swenson says. "You can never have too much ice, and it is devastating to run out."

Prep your drinks and garnishes. Measure out and prepare your ingredients as much as possible, and make sure everything is conveniently within reach, whether you're playing bartender or setting up an area where guests can serve themselves.

Although all the recipes in this book yield a single cocktail (unless otherwise specified), equal-parts drinks scale up with ease. That means the same drink you enjoy solo can be multiplied to serve two, or even become a punch- or pitcher-size drink for a group.

Florentina Duran, bar supervisor of LB Tavern at the Lord Baltimore Hotel, Baltimore, Maryland, relies on equal-parts drinks to speed drinks service. Although she's not exactly hosting a cocktail party, she's still hosting what amounts to a large group gathering in the high-volume bar space at a boutique hotel.

"If you want consistency, equal parts is the way to go," she advised. "It's so much easier. I usually pre-make the cocktail, because when you're rushing, it never tastes the same." (Try Duran's La Ciudad cocktail, page 68.)

In addition, the equal-parts template offers an unforeseen advantage: You can use pretty much any container to portion out ingredients for big batches. "You don't *have* to use a measuring cup!" one friend gleefully pointed out. "You could use a Quaker Oatmeal can, as long as you use it for all the ingredients, it's still equal parts." I hadn't thought of that particular scenario, but my whimsical friend makes a good point.

The one exception to the rule when scaling up drinks: Use a lighter hand when adding bitters, since they can overwhelm a drink in larger quantities. Add about half of what's called for in the recipe, then taste the drink, and add more if you like.

PARTY-SIZE DRINKS

For your next party, try making a big batch of one of the following drinks. They scale up well, so you can make them before your guests arrive, allowing you to enjoy your party instead of getting trapped behind the bar.

Bottled Cocktails

In general, spirit-forward cocktails (which contain little or no juice) work best for bottled drinks.

For example, try this template for a drink containing three ingredients. In a large pitcher, combine equal parts (about 2 cups [480 ml]) of each ingredient, plus ½ cup [120 ml] water (this mimics the dilution that ice would provide) to end up with about 6½ cups [1.5 L].

Stir to combine, and decant into two clean wine bottles. Chill the bottles in the refrigerator for two hours. When ready to serve, pour directly into coupe glasses, with no additional ice. Serves 10 to 12.

Try these drinks as bottled cocktails:

- En Cuarto (page 102)
- Negroni (see page 60)
- The Paper Plane (page 112)
- Rob Roy (page 46)
- Trident (page 74)
- Water Lily (page 104)

Pitcher or Punch-Bowl Cocktails

Cocktails with lots of fruit and fizz are relatively forgiving in pitcher or punch format.

Pitcher Cocktails In a large pitcher (or divided evenly among two smaller pitchers), combine equal parts of each ingredient to make about 6½ cups [1.5 L] and stir to combine. Add the ice at the very last minute (or scoop ice directly into glasses instead of the pitcher) to avoid watered-down drinks, and stir again to chill. Serves 10 to 12.

Punch-Bowl Cocktails Make a big block of Punch-Bowl Ice (see right) at least one day before the party. Just before the party, combine equal parts of each ingredient to

make about 6½ cups [1.5 L] in a punch bowl, and stir to combine. Add the ice at the last minute, plus a ladle to serve the drinks. Serves 10 to 12.

Try these drinks as pitcher or punch-bowl cocktails:

- Americano/Vespucci (page 34)
- Cucumber Gimlet (page 72)
- The Hudson Mule (page 64)
- Paloma (page 118)
- Rum Punch (page 122)

Punch-Bowl Ice

If you're transforming an equal-parts drink into a punch, don't use ice cubes in the punch bowl. They will melt quickly and water down the drink. Instead, use large blocks of ice, which will melt slowly over the course of an evening.

Since this ice will eventually mix with the drinks, consider using bottled or filtered water if the quality of your tap water isn't ideal. For crystal-clear ice, use distilled or boiled water. When selecting a container for freezing the ice, the key is go as big as possible while still leaving room in the punch bowl to maneuver the ladle.

Simple Punch-Bowl Ice At least one day in advance, pour water into disposable aluminum loaf pans, filling them about halfway, or disposable aluminum pie pans, filling almost completely, and freeze until completely firm. When you're ready to serve, peel the pan away. Alternatively, use a bowl to create rounded ice. Run the bottom of the bowl under hot water briefly to release the ice.

Decorative Punch-Bowl Ice Use a whimsically shaped Bundt pan or a tube pan. At least one day in advance, fill the pan with water and freeze until completely firm. When you're ready to serve, run the bottom of the pan under hot water briefly to release the ice.

TWO EQUAL PARTS

Think 50-50 Martinis, classic Americanos, and sherry-soaked Bamboo Cocktails. These streamlined two-ingredient drinks are pared down to the crisp essentials, but still offer plenty of flavor.

50+50 Martini

DRY GIN + DRY VERMOUTH

Equal parts gin and dry vermouth was the standard pre-Prohibition martini proportion, although it's more common now to find the vermouth dialed down to the bare minimum. The 50-50 still deserves some love; dress it up with an olive to accentuate vermouth's sweet-savory profile.

In an ice-filled mixing glass, combine the gin and vermouth. Stir well, and strain into a chilled martini glass. Garnish with the olive before serving.

ICE CUBES

1½ OZ [45 ML]
DRY GIN

1½ OZ [45 ML]
DRY VERMOUTH

GREEN OLIVE
FOR GARNISH

Fifty-Fifty Martini

Audrey Saunders, co-owner of New York's famed Pegu Club, gets credit for reviving this martini style, tweaking it, and giving it a saucier name. She warns that not all gin/vermouth pairings are harmonious. One she likes is Tanqueray/Noilly Prat. Try this variation for extra citrusy aromatics. In an ice-filled mixing glass, combine 1½ oz [45 ml] each gin and dry vermouth, plus 2 dashes orange bitters. Stir well, and strain into a chilled martini glass. Garnish with a lemon peel before serving.

Americano

CAMPARI + SWEET VERMOUTH

This classic Italian cocktail dates back to Milan's Caffè Camparino in the 1860s, where it was known as the "Milano-Torino" (the Campari came from Milan, the sweet vermouth from Turin). Yet, its popularity with American expats soon gave rise to a new nickname for the drink: the Americano.

In an ice-filled rocks glass, combine the Campari and vermouth. Stir well, top with soda water, and garnish with the lemon twist before serving.

The Vespucci

This Americano-style variation is credited to Jonathan Russell, at New York's Blenheim restaurant. In an ice-filled rocks glass, combine 1½ oz [45 ml] each fino sherry and sweet vermouth, plus 3 or 4 dashes of birch bitters (or Angostura bitters). Stir well, and top with a splash of seltzer before serving.

ICE CUBES

1½ OZ [45 ML]
CAMPARI

1½ OZ [45 ML]
**SWEET
VERMOUTH**

SODA WATER
TO TOP

LEMON TWIST
FOR GARNISH

Mango Soju-tini

SOJU + MANGO JUICE

This versatile drink can be customized depending on what fruit juices you have on hand. Danny Lee, the owner of Mandu, a modern Korean restaurant in Washington, D.C., makes variations using aloe, grape, mango, peach, pineapple, orange, pear, even yogurt. If you're not familiar with soju, it's a Korean spirit traditionally made from rice. The flavor is relatively neutral—some liken it to that of vodka—although the alcohol level is about half of vodka, which makes this drink a relatively mild sipper.

Pour the soju into an ice-filled cocktail shaker. Shake vigorously to chill. Add the mango juice, and shake briefly to combine. Strain into a large martini glass and add the soda water before serving.

3½ OZ [105 ML]
SOJU

ICE CUBES

3½ OZ [105 ML]
**FRESH
MANGO JUICE**

SPLASH OF
SODA WATER

Midway Fuji

GIN + SAKE

Two crisp, aromatic ingredients in equal parts yield a harmonious, refreshing aperitif. Courtesy of Michael Lomonaco, Center Bar, New York, New York.

In an ice-filled cocktail shaker, combine the gin and sake. Shake vigorously and strain into a chilled coupe glass. Garnish with the cucumber before serving.

ICE CUBES

1½ OZ [45 ML] **GIN**

1½ OZ [45 ML] **SAKE**, SUCH AS JUNMAI-SHU

THIN RIBBON OF CUCUMBER THREADED ON A TOOTHPICK FOR GARNISH

Bamboo Cocktail

DRY SHERRY + DRY VERMOUTH

This classic cocktail was created in the 1890s by Louis Eppinger, manager of the Grand Hotel, Yokohama, Japan, to serve to visiting dignitaries. The symmetry of this drink is admirable—even two types of bitters, dashed out in equal proportion.

In an ice-filled mixing glass, combine the sherry, vermouth, and both bitters. Stir for 20 to 30 seconds until well chilled, then strain into a chilled coupe glass. Garnish with the orange twist before serving.

The Adonis

New York bartender and sherry-phile Dan Greenbaum shared this Bamboo riff, which features the light, mineral-like flavor of fino sherry, although he says that manzanilla works well too. In an ice-filled mixing glass, combine 1½ oz [45 ml] each fino sherry and sweet vermouth, plus 2 dashes orange bitters. Stir well, and strain into a chilled coupe glass. Garnish with a lemon twist before serving.

ICE CUBES

1½ OZ [45 ML]
DRY SHERRY

1½ OZ [45 ML]
DRY VERMOUTH

2 DASHES
ORANGE BITTERS

2 DASHES
ANGOSTURA
BITTERS

ORANGE TWIST
FOR GARNISH

The Highball

Once you've mastered drinks made with two equal parts, it's time to give the highball a try. Also made (usually) with two ingredients, the highball is a spectacularly straight-forward drink—a modest amount of spirit topped with lots of nonalcoholic sparkle, with perhaps a squeeze of citrus for good measure. And that easy template gives plenty of room to riff.

In its most basic format, that includes classics like the gin and tonic, vodka-soda or whiskey-soda, and the Jack and Ginger (Jack Daniels whiskey and ginger ale). Just add a scoop of ice, no measuring required.

Of course, bartenders are finding fresh ways to elevate the highball, such as using artisanal or regional sodas. Some bars (like Trick Dog in San Francisco) have gone so far as to dedicate entire sections of their menus to the highball format, or have pre-mixed highballs ready to serve on tap.

"With highballs, there's no way to mess this up," insists Morgan Schick of Trick Dog, who encourages would-be highball makers to haunt local-minded markets to find unusual sodas to inspire and mix. Here are three ideas to get you started.

ROOT BEER AND AMARO

From Morgan Schick, Trick Dog,
San Francisco, California

Pour one part (1½ oz [45 ml])
amaro (Trick Dog uses Averna)
into a highball glass, followed
by two parts (3 oz [90 ml])
root beer, or more if desired
(Trick Dog uses a craft root beer
called Dang). Scoop in ice, and
finish with a squeeze of lime. Drop
the spent lime shell into the drink
before serving.

A DAY AT THE RACES

From Karl Goranowski, Playground
Bar & Lounge, Tucson, Arizona

Pour one part (1½ oz [45 ml])
Irish whiskey (such as Jameson)
into a highball glass, followed
by three parts (4½ oz [135 ml])
lemon-lime soda (Goranowski
prefers Bundaberg, an Australian
brand) and a couple of dashes of
allspice dram (Angostura bitters
works, too). Garnish with a mint
sprig before serving.

CEL-RAY AND AQUAVIT

From Morgan Schick, Trick Dog,
San Francisco, California

Pour one part (1½ oz [45 ml])
aquavit into a highball glass,
followed by two parts (3 oz
[90 ml]) **Cel-Ray** (a celery-
flavored soda), or more if desired.
Scoop in ice. Garnish with a
cucumber spear before serving.

Hanky Panky

GIN + SWEET VERMOUTH

A classic cocktail—essentially an equal-parts martini that's given a brisk, bitter edge thanks to a couple of dashes of Fernet Branca, a particularly intense amaro.

In an ice-filled mixing glass, combine the gin, vermouth, and Fernet-Branca. Stir well, and strain into a chilled coupe glass.

Twist the orange peel over the drink to spray its essential oils over the top, run the peel around the rim of the glass, then drop in the peel before serving.

ICE CUBES

1½ OZ [45 ML]
GIN

1½ OZ [45 ML]
SWEET VERMOUTH

2 DASHES
FERNET-BRANCA

1 STRIP
ORANGE PEEL

Rob Roy

SCOTCH WHISKY + SWEET VERMOUTH

This drink, a variation on the classic Manhattan, isn't always served as an "equal parts" drink; often the ratio is two parts Scotch to one part vermouth. That said, this equal-parts version works remarkably well, especially if you prefer a slightly sweeter and less potent pour. However you choose to make yours, be sure to toast the Waldorf Astoria Hotel in New York, where the drink was created in 1894.

In an ice-filled mixing glass, combine the Scotch, vermouth, and bitters. Stir well, and strain into a martini glass. Garnish with the cherries before serving.

ICE CUBES

1½ OZ [45 ML] **SCOTCH WHISKY**

1½ OZ [45 ML] **SWEET VERMOUTH**

1 OR 2 DASHES ANGOSTURA BITTERS

BRANDIED CHERRIES (PAGE 22) SPEARED ON A TOOTHPICK FOR GARNISH

Blood Orange Caipirinha

CACHAÇA + BLOOD ORANGE JUICE

The national cocktail of Brazil gets an upgrade with vibrantly hued blood orange juice—but if that's unavailable, try grapefruit or regular orange juice instead.

In an ice-filled cocktail shaker, muddle the sugar and lime. Add the cachaça and orange juice. Shake well, pour into a large rocks or highball glass, and garnish with the orange peel, if desired, before serving.

ICE CUBES

1 TSP SUGAR

1 LIME, QUARTERED

2 OZ [60 ML] **CACHAÇA**

2 OZ [60 ML] **BLOOD ORANGE JUICE**

ORANGE PEEL FOR GARNISH (OPTIONAL)

Dandy Cocktail

RYE WHISKEY + SWEET VERMOUTH

A classic cocktail from *The Savoy Cocktail Book*, you don't see this one on too many cocktail menus. I blame the fact that the specs call for Dubonnet Rouge, which I've always found disappointing. This drink improves considerably with sweet vermouth, or a good red wine–based aperitif (such as Cocchi Torino or Lillet Rouge).

In an ice-filled mixing glass, combine the rye, vermouth, orange liqueur, and bitters. Stir until well chilled, then strain into a coupe glass. Twist both citrus peels over the glass to express the essential oils, then drop the peels into the glass and serve.

ICE CUBES

1½ OZ [45 ML]
RYE WHISKEY

1½ OZ [45 ML]
SWEET VERMOUTH
OR APERITIF WINE

3 DASHES
ORANGE LIQUEUR

DASH OF
ANGOSTURA
BITTERS

ORANGE AND
LEMON PEELS
FOR GARNISH

THREE EQUAL PARTS

It's astonishing what a simple trinity
of ingredients can provide. Although the
crimson, bitter-edged Negroni remains
the reigning three-part champ, just see
what the power of three can do for a
refreshing, effervescent highball like
The Hudson Mule or the creamy,
dessert-like Grasshopper.

La Louisiane

RYE WHISKEY + SWEET VERMOUTH + BENEDICTINE

This historic cocktail is at its best in New Orleans—the bar at Commander's Palace makes a particularly delightful version. It's a showcase for two Louisiana products: Herbsaint (although herbal absinthe works too) and Peychaud's bitters. Although this drink works well in equal parts, some people prefer a heavier hand on the rye. Feel free to adjust for your personal preference.

Pour a little Herbsaint into a small rocks glass. Gently roll the glass to coat the interior with the liqueur. Pour out and discard any extra liqueur. Place the glass in the freezer to chill while you finish mixing the drink.

In an ice-filled mixing glass, combine the rye, vermouth, Benedictine, and bitters. Stir well, and strain into the prepared glass. Garnish with the cherries before serving.

HERBSAINT (OR ABSINTHE) TO RINSE THE GLASS

ICE CUBES

¾ OZ [20 ML] **RYE WHISKEY**

¾ OZ [20 ML] **SWEET VERMOUTH**

¾ OZ [20 ML] **BENEDICTINE**

2 OR 3 DASHES PEYCHAUD'S BITTERS

BRANDIED CHERRIES (PAGE 22) SPEARED ON A TOOTHPICK FOR GARNISH

Sangarita

LIME JUICE + SIMPLE SYRUP + BLANCO TEQUILA

This "visually gorgeous," margarita-style drink is a big brunch seller at New York restaurant Joe & Misses Doe, says bartender/co-owner Jill Dobias. She recommends using a dark, tannic wine such as Merlot, Malbec, or a rich Cabernet for the float.

You can skip the float if preferred, but the red wine tempers the drink's natural sweetness, while adding complexity and visual interest.

Pour salt into a shallow bowl or plate. Run the lime wedge halfway around the rim of a margarita glass or large wine goblet. Gently roll the moistened outer edge of the glass in the salt.

In an ice-filled cocktail shaker, combine the lime juice, simple syrup, and tequila. Shake well, and pour into the prepared glass. Pour red wine over the rounded bowl of a spoon to "float" it on top of the drink and garnish with the lime wheel before serving.

COARSE SALT
(LIKE KOSHER
SALT) TO RIM
THE GLASS

1 LIME WEDGE
TO RIM THE GLASS,
PLUS LIME WHEEL
FOR GARNISH

ICE CUBES

1½ OZ [45 ML]
LIME JUICE

1½ OZ ([45 ML]
SIMPLE SYRUP
(SEE PAGE 23)

1½ OZ [45 ML]
**BLANCO
TEQUILA**

RED WINE,
SUCH AS MERLOT,
MALBEC, OR
CABERNET
SAUVIGNON
TO FLOAT

Disco Ball

YELLOW CHARTREUSE + GREEN CHARTREUSE + MEZCAL

"It's a shot, not a cocktail," explains Ford Roberts of the Grape & Grain Exchange in Jacksonville, Florida, who first brought this drink to my attention. Although Grape & Grain pulls it from the tap, this is easy enough to stir multiple portions in a mixing glass—and then pour a round for friends.

In an ice-filled mixing glass, combine the Yellow Chartreuse, Green Chartreuse, and mezcal. Stir well, strain into a shot glass, and serve.

ICE CUBES

½ OZ [15 ML]
YELLOW CHARTREUSE

½ OZ [15 ML]
GREEN CHARTREUSE

½ OZ [15 ML]
MEZCAL

The Negroni

This drink has completely captured the bartender imagination, spurring more variations than any other drink—white Negronis, mezcal Negronis—entire menus and events celebrate this three-ingredient cocktail!

According to legend, the drink was created by Count Camillo Negroni in Florence, Italy, around 1920, when he ordered an Americano (see page 34) but demanded gin be swapped in for soda water. The drink is beautiful to behold, with a sophisticated, slightly bitter edge that makes it an ideal *aperitivo*.

Once you've mastered the basic Negroni, try other drinks in the same family.

NEGRONI

Pour one part (1 oz [30 ml]) each **gin**, **Campari**, and **sweet vermouth** into an old-fashioned glass with ice cubes. (Optional: Top up with soda water.) Stir well, and garnish with an orange peel before serving.

BOULEVARDIER

Pour one part (1 oz [30 ml]) each **bourbon**, **Campari**, and **sweet vermouth** into a mixing glass with ice cubes. Stir well, and strain into a coupe glass (or strain into a rocks glass over fresh ice, if preferred). Garnish with an orange slice or Brandied Cherry (page 22) before serving.

Note: Some people prefer this drink with a slightly more generous measure of bourbon.

OLD PAL

Pour one part (1 oz [30 ml]) each **rye whiskey**, **Campari**, and **dry vermouth** into an old-fashioned glass with ice cubes. Stir well, and garnish with a lemon twist before serving.

All three of these drinks scale beautifully for a large group. Batch equal measures of ingredients in a pitcher, and decant into a bottle. Cap tightly.

To serve, pour into glasses over ice, and stir to chill. "Up" drinks like the Boulevardier can be poured into a mixing glass with ice, then stirred and strained into coupe glasses.

Toffee Negroni

AGED RUM + AMONTILLADO SHERRY + APEROL

There's not really any candy in this drink, loosely modeled on the Negroni template (see page 60) and created by New York bartender Lynnette Marrero. But the rich, deep tones of aged rum combined with luscious amontillado really do evoke caramel and toffee without overt sweetness.

In an ice-filled mixing glass, combine the rum, sherry, and Aperol. Stir well, and strain into a rocks glass over a large cube of ice. Garnish with the grapefruit twist before serving.

ICE CUBES,
PLUS A LARGE ICE
CUBE OR SPHERE
FOR SERVING

1 OZ [30 ML]
AGED RUM

1 OZ [30 ML]
**AMONTILLADO
SHERRY**

1 OZ [30 ML]
APEROL

GRAPEFRUIT TWIST
FOR GARNISH

The Hudson Mule

VODKA + APPLE JUICE + GINGER BEER

This refreshing highball was created by Christopher James of The Ryland Inn, Whitehouse Station, New Jersey, to celebrate the autumn harvest. The original recipe was made with an apple-based vodka from Hudson Valley producer Tuthilltown Spirits.

In an ice-filled collins glass, combine the vodka, apple juice, and ginger beer. Garnish with the apple wheel before serving.

ICE CUBES

2 OZ [60 ML]
VODKA

2 OZ [60 ML]
UNFILTERED, ALL-NATURAL APPLE JUICE

2 OZ [60 ML]
GINGER BEER

APPLE WHEEL FOR GARNISH

Sin Cyn

CYNAR + SWEET VERMOUTH + SCOTCH WHISKY

The "Cyn" in this drink refers to Cynar, an Italian bitter made from artichokes (although another mild amaro could be substituted in a pinch). This drink nods to the classic Cin-Cyn (see variation), which in turn nods to the Negroni. Yet, this drink deserves to stand alone as more than just another Negroni knockoff; the Scotch whisky provides plenty of oomph and personality. Created by Paul Dellevigne of Philadelphia, Pennsylvania's Red Owl Tavern.

In an ice-filled mixing glass, combine the Cynar, vermouth, and Scotch. Stir well, and strain into a rocks glass over a large cube of ice. Garnish with the orange twist before serving.

ICE CUBES, PLUS ONE LARGE ICE CUBE OR SPHERE FOR SERVING

1 OZ [30 ML]
CYNAR

1 OZ [30 ML]
SWEET VERMOUTH

1 OZ [30 ML]
SCOTCH WHISKY

ORANGE TWIST FOR GARNISH

Cin-Cyn

In an ice-filled mixing glass, combine 1 oz [30 ml] each Cynar, sweet vermouth, and gin plus a dash of orange bitters. Stir well, and strain into a coupe glass. Garnish with an orange slice before serving.

La Ciudad

BLANCO TEQUILA + GINGER LIQUEUR + YELLOW CHARTREUSE

Creator Florentina Duran of LB Tavern at the Lord Baltimore Hotel, Baltimore, Maryland, says this drink started as a margarita; two relatively light, herbaceous liqueurs balance out with just a fast squeeze of lime.

In an ice-filled collins glass, combine the tequila, ginger liqueur, Yellow Chartreuse, and lime juice and stir. Garnish with the lime twist before serving.

ICE CUBES

1¾ OZ [55 ML]
BLANCO TEQUILA

1¾ OZ [55 ML]
GINGER LIQUEUR,
SUCH AS DOMAINE DE CANTON

1¾ OZ [55 ML]
YELLOW CHARTREUSE

SQUEEZE OF LIME JUICE

LIME TWIST FOR GARNISH

Bijou

GIN + GREEN CHARTREUSE + SWEET VERMOUTH

Bijou is French for "jewel," and this pre-Prohibition classic indeed glimmers in the glass like a precious trinket.

In an ice-filled mixing glass, combine the gin, Green Chartreuse, and vermouth. Stir well, and strain into a Nick and Nora glass or a coupe glass. Garnish with the cherries, if desired, before serving.

Bijou, Part Deux

Subbing dry vermouth for sweet allows for a more opalescent, herbaceous cocktail. In an ice-filled mixing glass, combine 1 oz [30 ml] each gin, Green Chartreuse, and dry vermouth. Stir well, and strain into a Nick and Nora glass or a coupe glass and serve.

ICE CUBES

---

1 OZ [30 ML]
GIN

---

1 OZ [30 ML]
GREEN CHARTREUSE

---

1 OZ [30 ML]
SWEET VERMOUTH

BRANDIED CHERRIES (PAGE 22) SPEARED ON A TOOTHPICK FOR GARNISH (OPTIONAL)

Cucumber Gimlet

VODKA + LIME JUICE + LEMONADE

If you don't have lemonade on hand, make your own using equal parts lemon juice and simple syrup (see page 23). Check your finished drink, and adjust with a touch more sweetener if it becomes too tart.

In a cocktail shaker, muddle two of the cucumber slices to crush them and release some of their juice. Add the vodka, lime juice, lemonade, and a handful of ice. Shake well, and strain through a mesh strainer into a rocks glass over fresh ice. Garnish with the remaining cucumber slice and the basil leaf before serving.

3 SLICES FRESH CUCUMBER, EACH ABOUT ¼ IN [6 MM] THICK

1 OZ [30 ML] **VODKA**

1 OZ [30 ML] **LIME JUICE**

1 OZ [30 ML] **LEMONADE**

ICE CUBES

BASIL LEAF FOR GARNISH

Trident

AQUAVIT + CYNAR + DRY SHERRY

Seattle cocktail enthusiast Robert Hess, best known in booze circles as "DrinkBoy," concocted this drink in 2000, riffing on the Negroni with far-flung ingredients (Spain's sherry, Italy's Cynar—a relatively gentle amaro—and Scandinavia's aquavit) with flavor profiles that closely approximated the strong/bitter/sweet trinity of the classic Negroni. Created when the current cocktail renaissance was still in its infancy, many regard this drink as rightfully belonging to the canon of "New Classic" cocktails.

The drink was popularized by the Zig Zag Café in Seattle. "It became so popular there," Hess recalls, "that the Zig Zag was soon going through more Cynar than all of the other bars in Washington State combined."

Like the Negroni, this drink scales well for pre-batched bottled cocktails.

In an ice-filled mixing glass, combine the aquavit, Cynar, sherry, and bitters. Stir well, and strain into a chilled coupe glass. Garnish with the lemon peel before serving.

ICE CUBES

1 OZ [30 ML]
AQUAVIT

1 OZ [30 ML]
CYNAR

1 OZ [30 ML]
DRY SHERRY

2 OR 3 DASHES
PEACH BITTERS

LEMON PEEL
FOR GARNISH

Parisian Blonde

JAMAICAN RUM + ORANGE LIQUEUR + HEAVY CREAM

Adapted from London barman Harry Craddock's 1930 classic *The Savoy Cocktail Book*, this drink has a pleasing tropical lilt. It's equally good straight up or poured over crushed ice and adorned with a paper umbrella for a tiki-style drink.

In an ice-cube-filled cocktail shaker, combine the rum, orange liqueur, and cream. Shake well, and strain into a collins glass or tiki mug over crushed ice. Garnish with a sprinkling of nutmeg before serving.

Alternate (classic) presentation: Strain into a coupe glass. Garnish with nutmeg.

ICE CUBES,
PLUS CRUSHED ICE

1 OZ [30 ML]
JAMAICAN RUM

1 OZ [30 ML]
ORANGE LIQUEUR

1 OZ [30 ML]
HEAVY CREAM

FRESHLY GRATED NUTMEG FOR GARNISH

Orange Whiskey Cocktail

BOURBON + ORANGE JUICE + SODA WATER

This vintage sipper is adapted from *Famous New Orleans Drinks and How to Mix 'Em*, a cheeky 1937 tome. Although bourbon or rye may be used, the author advises, "sidestep Scotch or Irish [whiskey]" for this drink. If a sweeter pour is preferred, add a dash of simple syrup (see page 23). Create an orange flag to garnish by wrapping an orange wheel around a Brandied Cherry (page 22) and spear through both with a toothpick to secure.

In an ice-filled cocktail shaker, combine the bourbon, orange juice, and bitters. Shake well, and pour into a rocks glass, including the ice (this works best if your rocks glass is on the larger side; otherwise opt for a highball glass). Top up with the soda water. Garnish with the orange flag and serve.

ICE CUBES

¾ OZ [20 ML]
BOURBON OR RYE WHISKEY

¾ OZ [20 ML]
ORANGE JUICE

DASH OF PEYCHAUD'S BITTERS

¾ OZ [20 ML]
SODA WATER

1 ORANGE FLAG (SEE HEADNOTE) FOR GARNISH

Brandy Alexander

BRANDY + DARK CRÈME DE CACAO + HEAVY CREAM

This cozy cocktail is popular as an after-dinner treat; in some circles, it's a popular holiday tipple as well.

This equal-parts recipe yields a creamy, dessert-worthy drink. Some people prefer a drier pour, with a heavier hand on the brandy; feel free to adjust for taste.

In an ice-filled cocktail shaker, combine the brandy, crème de cacao, and cream. Shake well, and strain into a martini glass or coupe glass. Garnish with a sprinkling of nutmeg before serving.

ICE CUBES

1 OZ [30 ML]
BRANDY

1 OZ [30 ML]
DARK CRÈME DE CACAO

1 OZ [30 ML]
HEAVY CREAM

FRESHLY GRATED NUTMEG FOR GARNISH

Grasshopper

GREEN CRÈME DE MENTHE +
WHITE CRÈME DE CACAO + HEAVY CREAM

This cool minty-green drink has had a renaissance among bartenders of late. It's an old-school drink, with its roots at Tujague's Bar in New Orleans, circa 1910, where it's still served today. The drink had a comeback in the 1950s, when it often was blended with ice cream. Modern iterations have pared the drink back to basics.

Although the drink typically is served without a garnish, feel free to gild the lily with dark chocolate shavings or a mint sprig.

In an ice-filled cocktail shaker, combine the crème de menthe, crème de cacao, and cream. Shake well, strain into a Nick and Nora glass or coupe glass, and serve.

ICE CUBES

1 OZ [30 ML]
GREEN CRÈME DE MENTHE

1 OZ [30 ML]
WHITE CRÈME DE CACAO

1 OZ [30 ML]
HEAVY CREAM

FOUR EQUAL PARTS

Like a four-part box step or a barbershop quartet, the following drinks work together in amazing harmony, from the old-school classic Corpse Reviver No. 2 to the wildly (and deservedly) popular Paper Plane.

Sunflower

GIN + LEMON JUICE + ST-GERMAIN
ELDERFLOWER LIQUEUR + ORANGE LIQUEUR

Super-easy—the glass gets a quick rinse of absinthe, then the remaining ingredients are measured out in equal parts to yield this sunny yellow sipper. Though Sam Ross, now of New York bar Attaboy, created this drink as an adaptation of the classic Corpse Reviver No. 2 (see page 106), it deserves a place of its own in the modern cocktail canon.

Pour the absinthe into a coupe glass. Gently roll the glass to coat the interior with the liqueur. Pour out and discard any extra liqueur.

In an ice-filled cocktail shaker, combine the gin, lemon juice, elderflower liqueur, and orange liqueur. Shake well, and strain into the prepared glass. Garnish with the lemon peel before serving.

ABSINTHE TO RINSE THE GLASS

ICE CUBES

¾ OZ [20 ML]
GIN

¾ OZ [20 ML]
LEMON JUICE

¾ OZ [20 ML]
ST-GERMAIN ELDERFLOWER LIQUEUR

¾ OZ [20 ML]
ORANGE LIQUEUR

LEMON PEEL FOR GARNISH

Mildred Pierce

MEZCAL + APEROL + GRAPEFRUIT LIQUEUR + LEMON JUICE

Courtesy of Abigail Gullo, of Compère Lapin, New Orleans, Louisiana. This also works with tequila, but the smokiness of mezcal adds a rougher edge to this rosy drink. It's pretty, but sure packs a punch!

In an ice-filled cocktail shaker, combine the mezcal, Aperol, grapefruit liqueur, and lemon juice. Shake well, and strain into a chilled Nick and Nora glass. Garnish with the lemon twist before serving.

ICE CUBES

¾ OZ [20 ML]
MEZCAL

¾ OZ [20 ML]
APEROL

¾ OZ [20 ML]
GRAPEFRUIT LIQUEUR,
SUCH AS GIFFARD PAMPLEMOUSSE ROSÉ

¾ OZ [20 ML]
LEMON JUICE

LEMON TWIST FOR GARNISH

Sharpie Mustache

RYE WHISKEY + DRY GIN +
MELETTI AMARO + BONAL

Created by bartender Chris Elford for bitters-centric New York bar Amor y Amargo, this drink is bitter and boozy by design, but also offers layers of herbs and spices that some have likened to the familiarity of cola. It drinks smoother and easier than you might expect.

This is one of the few drinks I've seen served in a rocks glass without the rocks (ice).

In an ice-filled mixing glass, combine the rye, gin, amaro, Bonal, and bitters. Stir well, and strain into a chilled rocks glass. Garnish with the orange peel before serving.

ICE CUBES

¾ OZ [20 ML]
RYE WHISKEY

¾ OZ [20 ML]
DRY GIN

¾ OZ [20 ML]
MELETTI AMARO

¾ OZ [20 ML]
BONAL
(AN APERITIF WINE; SWEET VERMOUTH MAY BE SUBSTITUTED)

2 DASHES BITTERMENS 'ELEMAKULE TIKI BITTERS

ORANGE PEEL FOR GARNISH

Volstead

SIMPLE SYRUP + VODKA + ST-GERMAIN
ELDERFLOWER LIQUEUR + LEMON JUICE

The name is a wink-wink reference to the Volstead Act, which ushered in the dark time known in the United States as Prohibition. Created by mixologist Jeremy Strawn of New York bar Lazy Point, this crisp sipper is ideal for languorous summer days.

In a cocktail shaker, muddle four of the strawberries with the simple syrup. Add the vodka, elderflower liqueur, lemon juice, and a handful of ice. Shake well, and strain into a coupe glass. Top up with Prosecco, if desired, and garnish with the remaining strawberry on the rim of the glass before serving.

5 FRESH STRAWBERRIES

¾ OZ [20 ML] **SIMPLE SYRUP** (SEE PAGE 23)

¾ OZ [20 ML] **VODKA**

¾ OZ [20 ML] **ST-GERMAIN ELDERFLOWER LIQUEUR**

¾ OZ [20 ML] **LEMON JUICE**

ICE CUBES

PROSECCO TO TOP (OPTIONAL)

The Divine Lorraine

BOURBON + ST-GERMAIN ELDERFLOWER LIQUEUR + AMARO NONINO + SWEET VERMOUTH

I first sampled this bourbon-soaked sipper at the St. Charles Exchange, Louisville, Kentucky—spiritual home of all things bourbon—thanks to bartender Colin Shearn (now with Magnolia House in Pasadena, California).

In an ice-filled mixing glass, combine the bourbon, elderflower liqueur, amaro, vermouth, and orange cream citrate. Stir well, and strain into a chilled coupe glass. Garnish with the orange twist before serving.

—

ICE CUBES

—

¾ OZ [20 ML]
BOURBON

—

¾ OZ [20 ML]
ST-GERMAIN ELDERFLOWER LIQUEUR

—

¾ OZ [20 ML]
AMARO NONINO

—

¾ OZ [20 ML]
SWEET VERMOUTH

—

9 DROPS BITTERMENS ORANGE CREAM CITRATE (OR 3 DASHES ORANGE BITTERS)

—

ORANGE TWIST FOR GARNISH

The Last Word

If the Negroni is the number-one, equal-parts favorite of bartenders, the Last Word takes the number-two spot. Like the Negroni, it's a classic cocktail that has spawned dozens of riffs.

This four part-harmony cocktail hails from the Detroit Athletic Club in Detroit, Michigan, and is one of a small handful of drinks actually created during the Prohibition years. The cocktail is attributed to Frank Fogarty, described by some as "a very fine monologue artist." In fact, some say that's how the drink got its name; Fogarty always had the last word.

But the drink was lost to history until 2004, when Seattle barman Murray Stenson discovered it in Ted Saucier's classic cocktail book *Bottoms Up* and re-popularized the drink during his tenure at Seattle's Zig Zag Café. As the cocktail renaissance swept across the nation, it brought The Last Word back—including to Detroit's bar scene.

THE LAST WORD

From the Detroit Athletic Club, Detroit, Michigan

In an ice-filled cocktail shaker, combine equal parts (¾ oz [20 ml]) **dry gin**, **Green Chartreuse**, **Maraschino liqueur**, and **lime juice**. Shake well, and strain into a coupe glass. Garnish with a lime wheel before serving.

OH, MY WORD!

From Sother Teague, Amor y Amargo, New York, New York

In an ice-filled mixing glass, combine equal parts (¾ oz [20 ml]) **Old Tom gin**, **Amaro Montenegro**, **Green Chartreuse**, and **Maraschino liqueur**, plus a couple of dashes of lime bitters (Teague uses Scrappy's). Stir and strain into a coupe glass. Twist a lemon peel over the top of the drink to express the essential oils, then garnish the drink with the peel before serving.

THE FINAL WORD

From Phil Ward, Mayahuel, New York, New York

In an ice-filled cocktail shaker, combine equal parts (¾ oz [20 ml]) **rye whiskey**, **Green Chartreuse**, **Maraschino liqueur**, and **lemon juice**. Shake well, strain into a coupe glass, and serve.

THE LAST LAUGH

From Abigail Gullo, Compère Lapin, New Orleans, Louisiana. So named, Gullo says, because "the bubbles tickle your nose!"

In an ice-filled cocktail shaker, combine equal parts (¾ oz [20 ml]) **gin**, **Green Chartreuse**, **Maraschino liqueur**, and **lime juice**. Shake well, and strain into a champagne flute. Top with cava and garnish with a lime twist before serving.

Cran-Brandy Cobbler

BRANDY + CRANBERRY JUICE + SIMPLE SYRUP + LIME JUICE

This drink works best with unsweetened cranberry juice. If you're using a sweetened cranberry "cocktail," you may want to dial down the simple syrup a bit. Accompany with a straw for easy sipping.

In an ice-cube-filled cocktail shaker, combine the brandy, cranberry juice, simple syrup, and lime juice. Shake well, and strain into a julep cup or large rocks glass over crushed ice. Garnish with the mint sprig before serving.

Party size: For a larger group, mix the liquid ingredients in a bottle or pitcher ahead of time, but don't add ice. When serving, divide the crushed ice among the cups or glasses (it should nearly fill the glass), then pour the cocktail mix over the ice and garnish.

ICE CUBES,
PLUS CRUSHED ICE

1 OZ [30 ML]
BRANDY

1 OZ [30 ML]
**UNSWEETENED
CRANBERRY
JUICE**

1 OZ [30 ML]
SIMPLE SYRUP
(SEE PAGE 23) OR
ORANGE LIQUEUR

1 OZ [30 ML]
LIME JUICE

MINT SPRIG
FOR GARNISH

Far East Peach

RYE WHISKEY + MEZCAL + CRÈME DE PÊCHE + YUZU JUICE

Created by Steven Dragun of Brooklyn, New York, bar Lucey's Lounge, this jazzy sipper is made with yuzu, a mild citrus fruit from Japan. The drink is perfectly balanced with yuzu; if you're substituting lemon, consider using slightly less, since it can be more acidic.

In an ice-filled cocktail shaker, combine the rye, mezcal, crème de pêche, yuzu juice, and bitters. Shake well, and strain into a Nick and Nora glass. Garnish with the grapefruit peel before serving.

ICE CUBES

¾ OZ [20 ML]
RYE WHISKEY

¾ OZ [20 ML]
MEZCAL

¾ OZ [20 ML]
CRÈME DE PÊCHE

¾ OZ [20 ML]
YUZU JUICE

3 DASHES
BITTERMANS
TIKI BITTERS

GRAPEFRUIT PEEL
FOR GARNISH

En Cuarto

PISCO + DRY GIN + DRY VERMOUTH + SWEET VERMOUTH

Ivy Mix, proprietress of Brooklyn, New York's Leyenda, is all about spirits sourced from Latin America. This is how she approaches the martini—by incorporating pisco, a grape-based spirit made in Peru and Chile. In Spanish, the drink name means "in fourths" or "in quarters."

In an ice-filled mixing glass, combine the pisco, gin, and both vermouths. Stir well, and strain into a chilled martini glass. Garnish with the lemon twist before serving.

ICE CUBES

¾ OZ [20 ML]
PISCO

¾ OZ [20 ML]
DRY GIN

¾ OZ [20 ML]
DRY VERMOUTH

¾ OZ [20 ML]
SWEET VERMOUTH

LEMON TWIST
FOR GARNISH

Water Lily

GIN + ORANGE LIQUEUR +
CRÈME DE VIOLETTE + LEMON JUICE

This lovely lavender-hued drink was created for my friend Georgette by New York bartender Richie Boccato, during his tenure at famed speakeasy Milk & Honey. Georgette explains, "The 'Lily' was inspired by my middle name, Lillian, and the fact that when the ice floes are floating just so on top of the drink, it resembles the Monet masterpiece of the same name. And truth be told, I did used to drink them like water."

In an ice-filled mixing glass, combine the gin, orange liqueur, crème de violette, and lemon juice. Stir well, and strain into a coupe glass. Twist the orange peel over the drink to spray the oil over the top, then discard the peel before serving.

—
ICE CUBES

—
¾ OZ [20 ML]
GIN

—
¾ OZ [20 ML]
ORANGE LIQUEUR

—
¾ OZ [20 ML]
CRÈME DE VIOLETTE

—
¾ OZ [20 ML]
LEMON JUICE

—
1 THICK STRIP OF ORANGE PEEL

Corpse Reviver No. 2

DRY GIN + LILLET BLANC + ORANGE LIQUEUR + LEMON JUICE

This delicious gin sipper, credited to mixologist Frank Meier at the Ritz Bar in Paris in the 1920s, appears on the menu of any self-respecting speakeasy. But the rarely seen classic No. 1 is also an equal-parts drink.

In an ice-filled cocktail shaker, combine the gin, Lillet Blanc, orange liqueur, lemon juice, and absinthe. Shake well, strain into a coupe glass, and serve.

Corpse Reviver No. 1

In an ice-filled mixing glass, combine 1 oz [30 ml] each Cognac, Calvados (apple brandy), and sweet vermouth, plus 3 dashes Angostura bitters. Stir well, and strain into a coupe glass. Garnish with a Brandied Cherry (page 22) before serving.

ICE CUBES

¾ OZ [20 ML]
DRY GIN

¾ OZ [20 ML]
LILLET BLANC

¾ OZ [20 ML]
ORANGE LIQUEUR

¾ OZ [20 ML]
LEMON JUICE

DASH OF ABSINTHE

The Cornell Special

GIN + BENEDICTINE +
LEMON JUICE + CLUB SODA

Refreshing, bubbly and easy-drinking, this cocktail is adapted from Harry Craddock's 1930 classic *The Savoy Cocktail Book*. Although the classic presentation is straight up, it also works well served over ice, like effervescent lemonade.

In an ice-filled cocktail shaker, combine the gin, Benedictine, and lemon juice. Shake well, and strain into a coupe glass. Top up with the club soda and garnish with the lemon wedge before serving.

ICE CUBES

1 OZ [30 ML]
GIN

1 OZ [30 ML]
BENEDICTINE

1 OZ [30 ML]
LEMON JUICE

1 OZ [30 ML]
CLUB SODA
OR SPARKLING
MINERAL WATER

LEMON WEDGE
FOR GARNISH

The Sour

Although not strictly an "equal parts" cocktail, the sour has a satisfyingly straightforward ratio: One part sour (usually citrus juice), one part sweet (simple syrup, agave nectar, honey, or even orange liqueur), and usually two parts spirit, making a total of four parts. Sometimes an additional flavor—like fruit juice or a liqueur—is added as well.

The sour is the basic, versatile formula for so many classic drinks. With white rum, it becomes the daiquiri; with tequila, the margarita; with whiskey, the whiskey sour; with brandy, the sidecar.

Depending on your taste and the strength of your ingredients, you might want to tweak the proportions just a little so your drink is neither too tart nor too sweet (nor for that matter, too strong). But even those subtle modifications provide the backbone for a wide range of cocktails.

DAIQUIRI

In an ice-filled cocktail shaker, combine two parts (2 oz [60 ml]) **white rum**, one part (1 oz [30 ml]) **lime juice**, and one part (1 oz [30 ml]) **simple syrup** (see page 23). Shake well, and strain into a coupe glass. Garnish with a lime wedge before serving.

MARGARITA

If desired, moisten the edge of a rocks glass with a lime wedge, then roll the glass edge in coarse salt (like kosher salt).

In an ice-filled cocktail shaker, combine two parts (2 oz [60 ml]) **blanco tequila**, one part (1 oz [30 ml]) **lime juice**, and one part (1 oz [30 ml]) **sweetener** (divide between agave nectar and orange liqueur). Strain into a rocks glass, over fresh ice. Garnish with a lime wedge before serving.

WHISKEY SOUR

In an ice-filled cocktail shaker, combine two parts (2 oz [60 ml]) **bourbon**, one part (1 oz [30 ml]) **lemon juice**, and one part (1 oz [30 ml]) **simple syrup** (see page 23), plus a dash of Angostura bitters. Shake well, and strain into a rocks glass over fresh ice. Garnish with an orange slice and a Brandied Cherry (page 22) before serving.

SIDECAR

In an ice-filled cocktail shaker, combine two parts (2 oz [60 ml]) **brandy**, one part (1 oz [30 ml]) **lemon juice**, and one part (1 oz [30 ml]) **sweetener** (divide between simple syrup [see page 23] and orange liqueur). Strain into a coupe glass. Garnish with an orange twist before serving.

The Paper Plane

BOURBON + APEROL +
AMARO NONINO + LEMON JUICE

This "new classic" cocktail is credited to bartender Sam Ross, now with New York speakeasy Attaboy. Ideal as a nightcap, this has become a popular drink for bartenders to tweak, component by component (spirit, liqueur, amaro, citrus), often ending up with a very different final cocktail, as in the variation below.

In an ice-filled cocktail shaker, combine the bourbon, Aperol, amaro, and lemon juice. Shake well, strain into a coupe glass, and serve.

ICE CUBES

¾ OZ [20 ML]
BOURBON

¾ OZ [20 ML]
APEROL

¾ OZ [20 ML]
AMARO NONINO

¾ OZ [20 ML]
LEMON JUICE

Naked and Famous

Courtesy of Joaquin Simo, from New York bar Pouring Ribbons, this drink is made with ¾ oz [20 ml] each mezcal, Yellow Chartreuse, Aperol, and lime juice. Combine all the ingredients in an ice-filled cocktail shaker. "Shake it like you mean it," Simo urges, strain into a coupe glass, and serve.

FIVE EQUAL PARTS
AND MORE!

The following drinks incorporate five or more ingredients, all in a careful balancing act, ranging from The Morning Star, an autumnal apples-and-whiskey sipper, to festive, tropical Rum Punch.

The Morning Star

SWEET VERMOUTH + DRY VERMOUTH +
RYE WHISKEY + APPLE CIDER + ORANGE LIQUEUR